Marcel is a French mouse. He's a detective and he lives in Paris. But Marcel doesn't live in Paris *all* year. Every November he visits London. His old friend – Henry – has a small flat there.

Marcel loves London. The beautiful buildings . . . the big, black taxis . . . the museums and shops. He loves Paris, but he loves London too.

◆

This story is about one of Marcel's November holidays. It starts at three o'clock on a Tuesday afternoon. Marcel is walking from Knightsbridge station to Henry's flat. He has two heavy bags with him.

1

Henry's address is 42 Old Wilton Street. Marcel looks at the numbers – 36 – 38 – 40. Yes, here it is. Number 42.

He sees a sign. It says: 'Professor J. T. Barton'. Marcel looks at it and thinks, 'That's new.' Then he goes down to Henry's flat.

Henry opens the door and smiles.

'Marcel!' he says. 'Come in, come in!'

'Hello, Henry,' Marcel says. 'How are you?' (His English is very good.)

'I'm very well. And you?'

'Yes, thanks.'

'Good, good.' Henry takes Marcel's coat. 'Now,' he says, 'let's have some tea.'

The two friends sit in big chairs. They drink tea and talk.

At five o'clock Marcel says, 'There's a new person in number 42. What's his name? Burton? Barnam?'

'Barton,' Henry says. 'Professor Barton. He's very, *very* clever. And that's not all. After tomorrow he's going to be famous, too!'

'Famous?!' Marcel looks at his English friend. 'Why?'

'It's a very interesting story,' Henry says. 'He has some letters. They were under the floor of an old woman's house in Oxford.'

'And . . . ?' Marcel says.

'And they're from Shakespeare to his son,' Henry says.

'*Shakespeare!*'

'Yes.' Henry smiles. 'Shakespeare. The old lady telephoned Professor Barton, and the Professor visited her. They talked about the letters and she said, "I want to give them to the British Museum in London. Can you do that for me?" '

'And Professor Barton said yes?'

'That's right.'

'Where are the letters now?' Marcel asks.

'In the professor's flat. He's going to give them to the British Museum tomorrow morning at ten o'clock. A lot of journalists and TV people are going to be there.'

Suddenly there's a big *BANG!* and then a long *WHIZZZ!*

'What's that noise?' Marcel asks. He goes to the window. Then he remembers. 'Oh – fireworks. Of course, it's the 5th of November – your "Guy Fawkes Day".'

Then a man walks down the steps from 42 Old Wilton Street.

Marcel looks at him. 'Is that Professor Barton?' he asks.

'Yes,' Henry answers. 'He always goes to the cinema on Tuesday evenings.'

'Aha!' Marcel says.

'Why do you say "Aha!"?' Henry looks at his French friend. Then suddenly he understands. 'Oh, you want to look at the Shakespeare letters.' He smiles. 'OK. Why not?'

After tea the two mice visit Professor Barton's flat. There's a small hole near the front door. Henry stops in front of it.

'Here we are,' he says. 'Do you want to go in first?'

'No, no. After you,' Marcel says.

At 5.55 they're in the professor's flat. It's very big, with a lot of old chairs and books. There are some beautiful pictures, too.

'Come with me,' Henry says.

He walks across the floor. Then he starts to climb a very tall bookcase. Marcel is behind him. They go up and up and up for a long time. Then Marcel sits on Charles Dickens's book, *Little Dorrit*. He can hear a lot of fireworks in the street.

'*BANG! BANG! BANG!*' they go. '*WHEEE! POW! WHOOSH!*'

There's a small, white button in the bookcase. Henry smiles at Marcel, and presses it. Suddenly, some of the books start to move.

'Why are they moving?' Marcel says. Then he understands.

'Ah, I understand. There's a safe.'

'Yes,' Henry says. 'Now, you stay here. I'm going to open it.'

He takes some blue paper from his jeans. Then he climbs down to the safe. There are some numbers on the paper. He starts to read them. '55 – 14 – 62 – 29 – 8. Yes, that's right.'

After that, he puts his hands on the safe and moves the dial to the left. '55,' he says. Then he moves the dial to the right. '14.'

Suddenly there's a very, *very* big *BANG!!!*

'Wow!' Marcel says. 'That was a *big* firework.'

Henry doesn't stop. '62,' he says. '29. And . . . ' He moves the dial again. '. . . 8. There – that's it.'

He smiles at Marcel and opens the safe. But then suddenly his mouth falls open.

'Oh no!' he says.

'What's wrong?' Marcel asks.

'They're not here,' Henry says. 'The Shakespeare letters. They're not *here*!'

Marcel climbs down the bookcase and looks. His friend is right. The letters aren't in the safe. But that's not all. There's a big hole at the back of the safe, and a lot of smoke, too.

Marcel looks at Henry. Henry looks at Marcel. Then they climb into the safe.

'Look,' Marcel says. He can see a room in number 40 Old Wilton Street. He can see a person, too – a tall woman in a red dress. She's sitting at a table and talking on the telephone.

'Do you think . . . ?' Henry starts.

'Ssshh,' Marcel says. The two mice sit and listen.

'That's right,' the woman says. 'I'm going to New York. Yes, this evening.' She writes on a notepad. 'Thank you.' She puts down the telephone.

There's a bag on the bed in front of her. In it Marcel can see some letters. The woman closes the bag. After that, she walks to the door. She opens it, and then closes it behind her.

Henry looks at Marcel in the hot, dark safe. 'What are we going to do?' he asks. 'That woman's got the letters. Let's telephone the police.'

'No, there isn't time,' Marcel says. 'Do you know her?'

'The woman? No, I don't.'

'Who usually lives in that flat?'

'Two old women, but they're on holiday in Spain. Oh Marcel, what are we going to do?'

Marcel looks into the dark flat. 'Come with me,' he says.

He climbs into the old women's flat. Henry is behind him. The two mice run across the floor. Then they climb up a table. On the table there's a yellow light and a small, white notepad. Marcel looks at it under the light.

'What are you doing?' Henry asks.

Marcel doesn't answer. Then he says, 'Aha! I was right. Can you see?'

Henry smiles. 'Yes, I can. Not very well, but ... it says, *"Concorde – 7.20"*.'

Marcel puts down the notepad and looks at his watch. It's six o'clock. Then he starts to run down the leg of the table.

Henry runs down the leg of the table, too. 'Where are we going now?' he asks.

'Heathrow Airport, of course,' Marcel says.

At 6.05 the two mice are in Old Wilton Street. It's dark and cold. They walk quickly to Knightsbridge station. There are a lot of fireworks. '*BANG! WHEEE! POP! WHOOSH!*' Marcel watches them. Then he remembers the very big *BANG!!!* in the professor's flat.

'That was clever,' he thinks. 'Very, very clever.'

There are hundreds of people at Knightsbridge station. Marcel and Henry run under their legs and bags. Marcel can hear a noise.

'Quick, Henry,' he says. 'A train's coming.'

He's right. A train is coming into the station. A sign on the front of it says, 'Heathrow'. The doors open and the mice get on.

There are fifteen stations before Heathrow. Every time, the train stops. Henry says, 'Quick, quick – what are we waiting for?' Then the doors close and the train starts again.

At Heathrow the mice get off. Marcel looks left and right. 'Where do we go now?' he asks.

'I don't know,' Henry says. He looks left and right, too.

There are a lot of signs. Then suddenly Henry smiles. 'Marcel, look! That blue sign says "Concorde".'

'Good,' Marcel says. He looks at his watch. It's 7.10. 'Let's go,' he says.

The mice start to run again. 'Marcel,' Henry says, 'what are we going to do? OK, we find the woman . . . but then what do we do? How do we get the letters back?'

Marcel smiles. 'Wait and see,' he says.

They come to a door. It says, 'CONCORDE', but it's closed. Henry and Marcel stop in front of it.

'Oh no,' says Henry.

But then two men with big bags open the door and go in. The mice go in, too.

'Good,' Marcel says. He looks at the people in the room . 'Now ... can you see her?'

'No, I can't,' Henry says.

Marcel smiles. 'I can,' he says.

'Where?'

'There. In front of us.'

Henry looks. Marcel is right. The American woman is sitting on a chair and listening to her Walkman. She's reading a newspaper, too. Her bag is on the floor.

'OK – let's go,' Marcel says. He takes a small knife from his coat. 'Walk behind me, Henry – but be very, *very* quiet.'

He starts to walk across the room. Henry walks behind his friend. 'Marcel's a detective,' he thinks. 'It's going to be OK. He knows his job. He does this every day. Yes . . . it's – going – to – be – O – K.'

Marcel stops in front of the American woman's bag. He looks at Henry. 'Ssshh,' he says. 'Wait here.' Then he climbs up the bag.

After a short time he starts to make a hole in it with his knife. Henry watches. His mouth is open. He looks at the American woman. She's listening to music and reading. She doesn't look down.

Marcel climbs into the bag. It's dark. He closes his eyes and opens them again. Now he can see some jeans – a radio – some books. Then suddenly he sees the Shakespeare letters. 'Good,' he thinks.

He puts the letters on his back and starts to climb down again. Henry sees him and smiles. But then the mice hear a noise.

'*Bing bong!*'

The American woman looks at her watch. Then she takes off her Walkman and starts to put it in her bag.

'Hey!' she says. 'What . . . ? Two mice! What's this?'

'Quick, Henry – catch!' Marcel says. He gives the letters to Henry. Then he climbs down the bag. The mice run very quickly with the Shakespeare letters. They can hear the American woman behind them. She's running very quickly, too.

The door is open. A man is coming in. He's fat and he has two bags. The mice run under his legs. Then Marcel hears a big noise! He looks behind him. The American woman is on the floor, and the man is talking to her.

'Sorry,' he says. 'Are you OK?'

The woman stands up. 'No!' she says. Then she looks for the mice, but she can't see them.

At nine o'clock Marcel and Henry are back at Professor Barton's flat in Old Wilton Street. They're very happy. Marcel is sitting on the table. The Shakespeare letters are in front of him. He's reading them. Henry is standing at the window. He's watching the fireworks. Suddenly he sees a man in a brown coat. It's Professor Barton. He's coming home.

The professor is smiling. Then he walks into his flat and suddenly he stops smiling. Marcel and Henry are standing behind a chair. They watch him.

He goes to the safe. It's open. He looks in it and says, 'Oh no!'

Then he sees the Shakespeare letters on the table. 'But . . . ' He puts one hand on his head. 'I don't understand.' He looks at the safe. Then he looks at the letters – and then he looks at the safe again. 'Why are the letters here?' he says. 'When . . . ? How . . . ? I don't understand.'

In the morning, Henry and Marcel go to the British Museum. It's a cold day, and it's raining. In the museum there are a lot of journalists and TV people. They're waiting for Professor Barton. He arrives at ten o'clock.

'Good morning,' he says to them.

He starts to talk about the Shakespeare letters. Then he gives the letters to a man from the museum.

'Thank you very much, Professor,' the man says.

Henry and Marcel are standing at the back of the room. Henry smiles at his French friend.

'And thank *you*, Marcel,' he says.

ACTIVITIES

Before you read

1 Answer these questions. Find the words in *italics* in your dictionary. They are all in the story.

   a Which is not a job?

     detective   journalist   mouse   professor

   b Which two things can you hear?

     firework   sign   smoke   Walkman

   c Which can you climb up?

     bookcase   paper   steps   tea

   d Which do you press?

     button   dial   hole   safe

   e What can you do:

     – at a *museum*? – on a *notepad*?

2 Look at the pictures. What is this story about?

After you read

3 Finish these sentences about Marcel and Henry.

   a At three o'clock on Tuesday afternoon . . .

   b At 7.20 on Tuesday evening . . .

   c At nine o'clock on Tuesday evening . . .

   d At ten o'clock on Wednesday morning . . .

Writing

4 You are a journalist at the British Museum. Write five questions for Professor Barton.

5 You are the American woman. You have the letters and you are waiting for Concorde. Write your story.